PURSUIT!

GEORGINA PRESTON

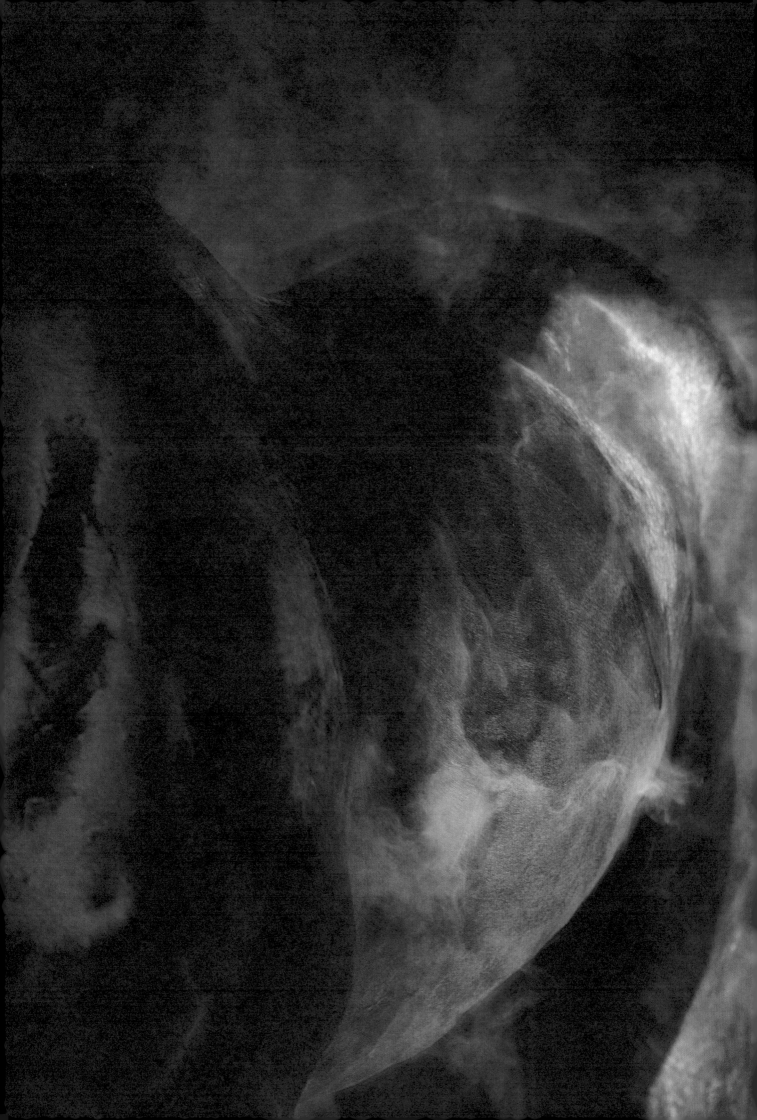

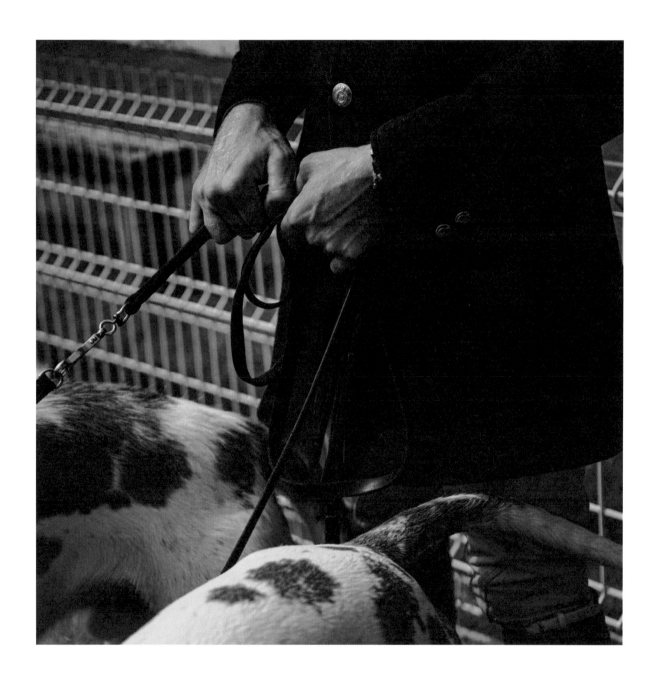

HUNTING WITH HOUNDS is an art form. Much has been written historically about foxhunting and the hunting of other quarry species with different types of hounds. Although outwardly much appears to remain the same today as it was centuries ago - with hunt staff and supporters continuing to wear traditional hunt dress and the hunting horn used to communicate with the hounds and the followers - the activities conducted by hunts in England, Wales and Scotland have adapted to comply with new and enforced legislation.

Traditional hunting, which was carried out by packs of Foxhounds, Harriers, Beagles, Basset hounds and other scent hounds, involved the hounds pursuing a live quarry. However, hunting became restricted in England and Wales following the passing of the Hunting Act 2004, which came into force on 18th February 2005. This law satisfied anti-hunting campaigners at the time it was passed, but there is much discussion about potentially "strengthening the Hunting Act" in future.

Hunting in Scotland changed following the implementation of the Protection of Wild Mammals (Scotland) Act 2002, which was subsequently repealed when further legislation was introduced on 3rd October 2023. Hunts operating in Scotland now require a licence to conduct wildlife management with a pack of hounds under the Hunting with Dogs (Scotland) Act 2023.

Foxhunting continues much as it always has done in the Republic of Ireland, whilst Northern Ireland is currently the only part of the UK where traditional quarry hunting with packs of hounds can continue. At the time of writing, it was expected that further proposals to change the existing law in Northern Ireland may be put forward, although a proposed bill to ban hunting with dogs in Northern Ireland was defeated in the Stormont Assembly in December 2021.

Ever-increasing urbanisation and different farming practices have meant that hunts have constantly had to adapt their lawful activities to ensure they can continue to exist when faced with adversity, and changes in legislation have been met in a similar proactive fashion. Today, the majority of packs in England and Wales take part in an activity called trail hunting, which replicates traditional methods, with the exception that the hounds pursue an artificial scent which has been laid across the countryside for them to follow, rather than them seeking out live quarry. There are some exemptions within the Hunting Act 2004 that enable some traditional hunting activity to continue, such as flushing to a bird of prey or guns.

Hunting activities may have evolved to ensure they remain compliant with the current law, but hunts and their followers continue to respect their heritage, which is so wonderfully showcased and celebrated in the pages of *Pursuit!*.

POLLY PORTWIN

Polly Portwin is a Director of the Campaign For Hunting at the Countryside Alliance and a journalist who has written for The Telegraph and Horse & Hound.

IT IS JUST AFTER 10 O'CLOCK on a Saturday morning, and the late November sun is shining on a muddy field in Wiltshire and a meet of the Duke of Beaufort's Hunt. Frankly, it could be any field anywhere in any county on any Saturday morning in late November, from the College Valley in Northumberland to the Cury Hunt who can, on a good day, see a storm brewing off the coast of Cornwall.

Hounds are already there with around forty mounted and more on foot. By quarter to eleven both numbers will have swelled. Within half an hour, when at last hounds move off, there might be, say, 200 mounted and a similar sized crowd gathered on the ground in waterproof hats and wellies and the sort of patterned tweed coat sold only at agricultural showgrounds. It's difficult to keep count of the numbers. Port is being served by the crate load and sausages from catering-issue tinfoil. This is a curiously old-fashioned sight, faintly bewildering to the novice and reassuringly familiar to everyone else which is, of course, the way everyone else really quite likes it to be. With some adjustments it could be 1824.

'You wouldn't think', said the lady from the VWH to a friend pointing out the liveries – the green of the Beaufort staff; the yellow-with-green-collar of the Berkeley; a cluster of visitors in red coats – 'that there was anything wrong'.

And then the horn is blown and horses and hounds start to move, slowly at first and then, in a short time, the air fills with the sound of galloping hooves and the song of foxhounds in cry. It is a remarkable, heart-stopping sight.

I'm glad Georgina has made this book. There is plenty of the picturesque from packs up and down the country, if not Albrighton to Zetland then a fair few in between and sideways, west, to Ireland with the Galway Blazers.

She has an eye for the quality of British tailoring, boot making and haberdashery. But what makes it distinctive is Georgina's commitment to the bigger picture, the whole package, the hard slog of kennels life from walking out at dawn to swabbing down at the end of the day. She's as happy knee deep in the charnel of the feed room as she is in the warmth of the tack room wood-burner, the febrile, tension-filled hothouse of the showring, or on the bitter cold winter mornings when nothing ever starts first time.

Foxhunters remain a species apart. They will live on baked beans or thin air in order to afford their sport. And as for sensible, I'm writing this in summer 2024 in the run-up to a General Election, which will likely see the landscape change again, but we, all of us, are counting down the days till it starts all over again. Perhaps a little like Daisy, Countess of Fingall, who when asked what one did in Meath in the summer replied, not missing a beat, 'we wait for winter'.

ROBIN MUIR

Robin Muir is a photographic historian and exhibitions arranger. As an external curator for the National Portrait Gallery, London, his most recent exhibition was Cecil Beaton's Bright Young Things (2020). A former Picture Editor of Vogue and the Sunday Telegraph Magazine, he is currently a Contributing Editor to Vogue and consultant to its archive of photographs and drawings. His survey of Vogue's historical engagement with royalty, The Crown in Vogue, was published in 2022.

This body of work is a collection of photographs taken over the past 10 years, a period during which my life has been deeply immersed in the world of hunting across the United Kingdom and Ireland. These photographs offer an affectionate documentation of this unique subculture from an intimate perspective. *Pursuit!* is an appreciation of a rural community with a rich tapestry of tradition, idiosyncrasies, and characters.

As a shy and introverted teenager, the hunting circle welcomed me with open arms. I befriended people from various walks of life, different social classes, ages, and socio-economic backgrounds, all united by a shared love and respect for the countryside. Among these people, both on and off the hunting field, I learned invaluable life skills and gained confidence. Hunting is more than the simplistic pursuit of a laid scent for hounds to follow; it unites people uniquely.

ACKNOWLEDGEMENTS

I'd like to thank:

My parents for facilitating my hunting addiction as a teenager, both financially and with their endless dedication to driving me around the countryside all winter — often picking me up from college with the trailer hitched up en route to a meet.

My grandfather, for always giving me his hand-me-down cameras and sternly reminding me that 'they are not toys!'

The Taunton Vale Foxhounds, for embracing me and my slightly out-of-control thoroughbred when we first appeared, and for becoming my extended family as I grew up. Also, for being so supportive of my elaborate ideas for the hunt newsletters, which eventually became books known as the 'Taunton Vale Flyers' - undoubtedly the predecessors to *Pursuit!*.

My photography tutors from my BA and MA at the University of the West of England (UWE Bristol): Jim Campbell, Shawn Sobers, Amanda Harman, Aaron Schuman, Amak Mahmoodian, and Lee Elkins, who have always left me inspired and confident after every conversation: I am so grateful for your unwavering support.

Robin Muir and Polly Portwin for taking the time to write their contributions to *Pursuit!* and their words of advice and guidance throughout this process.

Madeleine Bunbury, famous equestrian artist, whom I am lucky enough to have as a best friend. She whips me into shape every time I think about slacking and always believes in my projects and ideas with endless enthusiasm and positivity.

Anyone who has ever hired me for a commission or bought photographs from me — I would not have been able to pursue photography as my career without you.

All of the packs that have let me come along with my camera, and given me lifts on the back of their quads or in their Land Rovers, often accompanied by sausage rolls and flasks of coffee.

Lastly, a huge thank you to you for taking the time to look through this book. It has been an enormous labour of love and something that I am extremely proud of. This book is a reflection of all the incredible people who have shaped and influenced my path. I hope it does justice to the world of hunting, for which I have everlasting gratitude.

INDEX

PUBLISHED 2024
INFO@GEORGINAPRESTON.COM
WWW.GEORGINAPRESTON.COM

ISBN 978-1-3999-8929-9

9 781399 989299 >